# FUN WITH

**ALPHABET • LETTER SOUNDS AND BLENDS • CH, SH, AND TH WORDS**

QEB Publishing

Written by Ann Montague-Smith
Illustrated by Bill Bolton
Editorial Consultants: David and Penny Glover

Copyright © QEB Publishing, Inc. 2010
Published in the United States by
QEB Publishing, Inc.
3 Wrigley, Suite A
Irvine, CA 92618

A CIP record for this book is available from the Library of

Congress.

ISBN 978 1 59566 718 2

Printed in China

# Contents

# Suggestions for Using this Book

• Before reading this book, read the title and look at the front cover illustration with your child. Talk about the characters and what they are doing. Which character does your child think is Azlo? Can your child think of anyone he or she knows with a name beginning with the same letter as Azlo?

• Can your child think of anybody he or she knows with a name ending with the same end letter as Anzi?

• Can your child think of any words that rhyme with Blip?

• Can your child think of anyone he or she knows with a name beginning with the same letter as Meeble?

• Draw your child's attention to the beginning of words—e.g. "This word begins with an **n** (letter name) and it makes a **nnnnnn** sound." or "This word begins with an **s** (letter name) and an **h**. When we put them together, they make a **shhh** sound."

• When you are talking about letter sounds, try not to add too much of an **uh** sound. Say **mmm** instead of **muh**, **ssss** instead of **suh**. Saying letter sounds as carefully as possible helps children when they are trying to build up or spell words.

• Talk about the characters on each page—what they look like, what they are doing and why, and what they might be thinking.

• Encourage your child to express opinions and preferences—e.g. "Which picture do you like most?" "Which part of the book did you like best? Why?"

• Help your child to make up his or her own alphabet book called "[Your child's name] ABC." Think of a word for each letter. Say the name and sound of each letter as you write it down with the word. Your child might like to draw a picture for each one.

• Read, read, read. Read aloud with children every day. As children learn phonetic rules, show them where they appear in the stories you read.

• Say the sound of a letter and ask your child to go on a word hunt to find words in the book that begin with that sound. For the letter b, for example, your child might find "bang" and "bed" on page 11, "ball" on page 13, and "bone" on page 27.

• Talk about words: their meaning, how they sound, how they look, and how they are spelled. However, if your child gets restless or bored, stop. Enjoyment of the book or activity is essential if we want children to grow up valuing books and reading!

• Make word searches with sight words for children to complete.

• Do not feel the need to correct every word a child misreads. When reading for fun, avoid corrections at all. Reading should involve as little stress as possible to encourage a child to read.

•Read more than just books. Look at labels and signs and particularly of things children are familiar with. Help them to sound out the letters in these words as well.

• Celebrate a sound of the day. Do activities, read books, and eat foods that have a particular sound in them. Write about what you have done to reinforce the use of letters to represent sounds.

• Read books such as those written by Dr Seuss to practice phonics and sounding out words.

• Use the Internet to locate high-frequency words by year group. These words are those that children will see most frequently. Turn these words into flash cards and practice them often.

• Do not simply teach the sight words in isolation. Show them to children as they appear in text.

• Help children make songs with sight words that they can sing for fun. Write the lyrics so children can read along.

• On the first or second re-reading, leave out some of the words being used to illustrate the letter sounds and let your child say them. Point to the illustration to help your child supply the word.

• Make two sets of sight word flash cards. Use them to play matching games.

• As you read the book to your child, run your finger along underneath the text. This will help your child follow the reading and focus on how the words both look and sound.

• Choose any page and use the illustration to play "I Spy," using letter sounds rather than names.

Azlo is learning the alphabet!

Find out what funny things he finds for every letter.

What words can you think of for each letter of the alphabet?

# Learn the Alphabet with Azlo

C is for the **caterpillar** crawling up my wall.

12

**D** is for the **dog**
that ran off with my ball.

E is for the "elephant" that stepped upon my toe.

F is for the **funny face**
that I drew in the snow.

G is for the **goat** that
eats everything in sight.

H is for the **hat** that's jammed on really tight.

I is for the **insect** that's landed on my nose.

J is for all the **juice** that I spilled on my clothes.

K is for my **kitten** that's sitting on my knee.

L is for the **lion** that's chasing after me.

19

M is for
the **monkey**
with little dancing feet.

N is for the
**nuts** that the
squirrel likes
to eat.

**O** is for the **octopus** that invited me for tea.

21

P is for the **pirate** who took me out to sea.

**Q** is for the **queen** who is making apple pie.

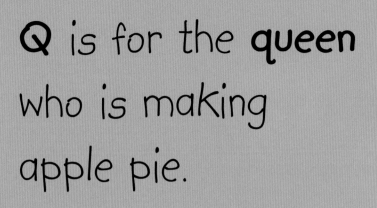

**R** is for the *rainbow*

stretched across the sky.

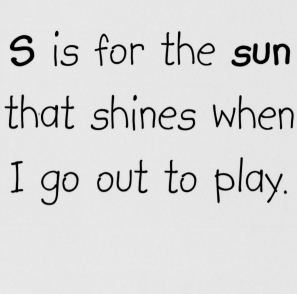

**S** is for the **sun** that shines when I go out to play.

T is for the **tiger** that made me run away.

**U** is for the **umbrella**
that I need in the rain.

**V** is for the **vase**
I broke playing
with my plane.

**Y** is for the **yogurt** I'm eating in this tree.

Z is for the **zebras** that like to play with me.

# Beginning Sounds

Now you've learned the alphabet with Azlo, can you work through these puzzles?

**The beginning sound is the sound a word starts with. It is the first sound you say.**

The letter b is the first sound in…

The letter c is the first sound in…

The letter d is the first sound in…

The letter f is the first sound in…

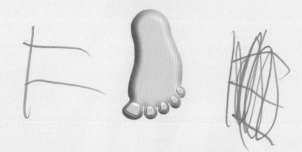

The letter g is the first sound in…

The letter h is the first sound in…

**Letter bank**

| b | c | d |
|---|---|---|
| f | g | h |

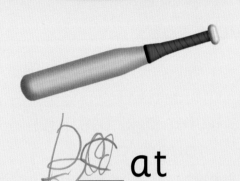

__at

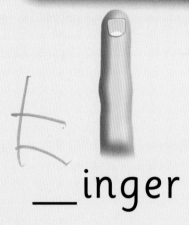

__inger

__ow

__irl

__uck

__en

# Ending Sounds

**The ending sound is the sound a word ends with. It is the last sound you say.**

The letter n is the last sound in...

The letter p is the last sound in...

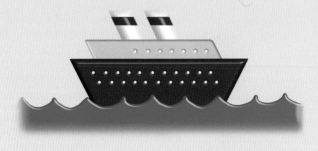

The letter r is the last sound in...

The letter t is the last sound in...

**Point to the correct ending sound for each picture below.**

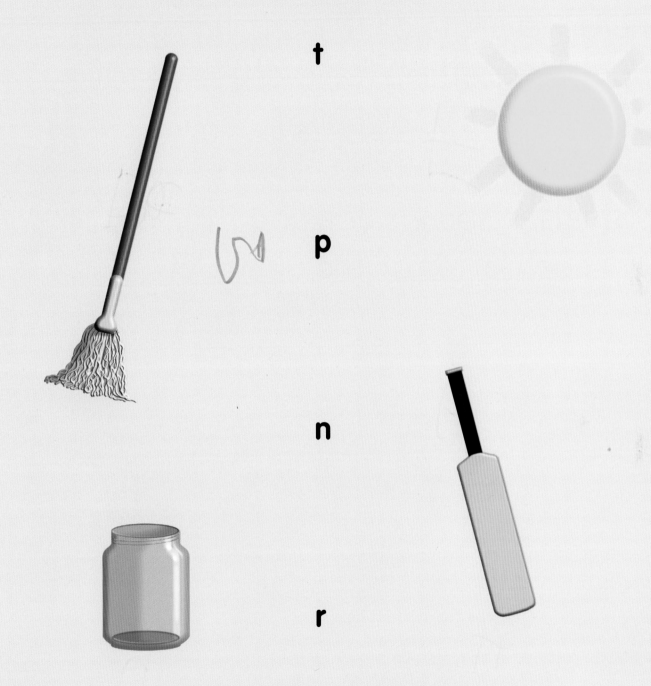

t

p

n

r

Anzi is learning letter sounds!

There were lots of funny things at her party—something for every letter of the alphabet.

What letter sounds can you think of for each letter of the alphabet?

# Learn Letter Sounds with Anzi

When **A**nzi gave a party for the monsters, there were **a**nimal **a**crobats,

**b**ig **b**lue **b**alloons for **b**aby monsters,

**e**xcellent **e**gg salad sandwiches

for the **fl**ying **f**airy,

**g**hosts with **g**uitars,

hats with hearts
and holly,

immense insects

and jiggly Jell-O,

king-size **k**iwi fruits

and **l**ots of **l**emon soda,

43

nuts to nibble,

**o**ranges and
**o**melets,

pizzas

and pies,

quilts for **q**uiet snoozes,

48

rabbits riding a reindeer,

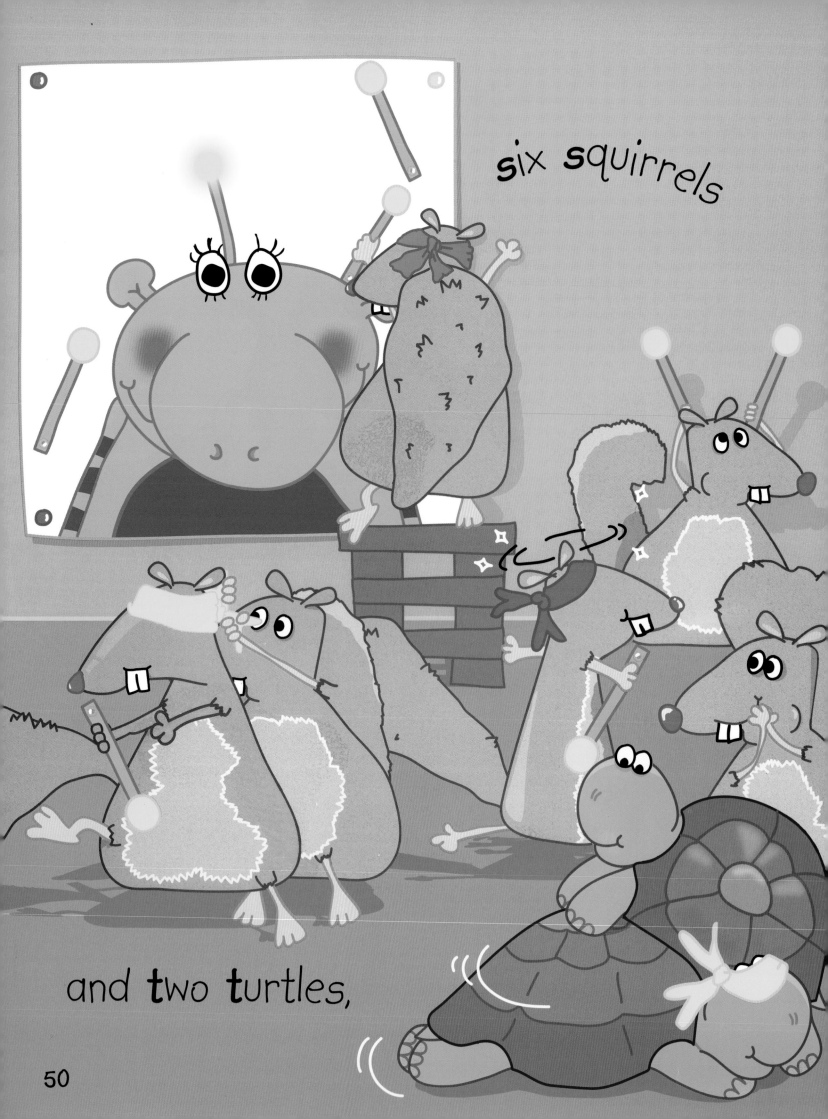

six squirrels

and two turtles,

50

uncles under umbrellas

and a vulture with a violet violin,

51

walruses in wooly wigs,

extra **y**ogurts for the **z**ebra,

and monsters in masks marching to music...

54

until they went to bed!

# Sounds Together

Now you've learned letter sounds with Anzi, can you work through these puzzles?

By putting together beginning and ending sounds, you can make words.

The letter j is
the first sound in…

The letter k is
the first sound in…

The letter l is
the last sound in…

The letter s is
the last sound in…

The letter w is
the first sound in…

The letter y is
the first sound in…

# Unusual Letters

**Some letters are not used very often.**

The letter q is the first sound in…

The letter q is almost always followed by u. When you say the letters qu, you say the sound kw.

The letter x is the last sound in…

Sometimes x sounds like ex.
Sometimes it sounds like a z.
Sometimes it sounds like ks.

**Point to the pictures that use qu, then to the pictures that use x.**

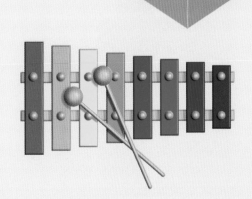

# Short Vowels

Vowels make different sounds. Sometimes vowels make a short sound.

**Short a sound**

cap

**Short e sound**

hen

**Short i sound**

pin

**Short o sound**

frog

**Short u sound**

bug

# Long Vowels

Some vowels have a long sound. The e at the end of the word is silent, but it tells you that the vowel before it has a long sound.

**Long a sound**

cape

**Long e sound**

here

**Long i sound**

bike

**Long o sound**

smoke

**Long u sound**

flute

Blip is learning letter blends!

Find out what words with letter blends are on his shopping list.

What words can you think of with letter blends?

# Learn Letter Blends with Blip

A **cr**own for the **cr**ocodile

A **dr**um and a **dr**agon

# Fruit for my frog

# Grapes for Grandpa

A **present** for the **princess**

A **tr**ain and a **tr**umpet

# A **cl**oak for the **cl**own

A **fl**ag and some **fl**owers

Some **gl**oves and some **gl**itter

Plenty of plums and plants

A **sl**ed and a **sl**ide

# A **sc**arf for **sc**hool

# A **sk**ateboard for the **sk**eleton

Some **sn**owdrops and a **sn**ake

Spoons for the spider

**St**amps and a **st**arfish

79

A **sw**ing for the **sw**an ...

# Consonant Blends

Now you've learned letter blends with Blip, can you work through these puzzles?

Consonant blends have two or three consonants. Each consonant makes a sound. The sounds join together.

b + l make
the sound in...

c + r make
the sound in...

c + l make
the sound in...

d + r make
the sound in...

f + l make
the sound in...

g + r make
the sound in...

p + l make
the sound in...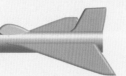

s + n make
the sound in...

s + t make
the sound in...

s + p + r make
the sound in...

**Letter bank**

| cl | cr | cr | dr |
|----|----|----|----|
| gr | fl | br | pl |

___oom

___ow

___oth

___y

___op

___y

___in

___ant

Meeble is learning ch, sh, and th words!

Find out what funny things she
has in her magic box.

What words can you think of that
begin with ch, sh, and th?

# Learn ch, sh, and th Words with Meeble

What's in Meeble's magic box today?

87

# What's in Meeble's magic box today?

What's in Meeble's magic box today?

# What's in Meeble's magic box today?

What's in Meeble's magic box today?

What's in Meeble's magic box today?

97

# What's in Meeble's magic box today?

What's in Meeble's magic box today?

# What's in Meeble's magic box today?

A **sh**y little **sh**ark!

Hooray!

Hooray!

# What's in Meeble's magic box today?

# Consonant Pairs

Now you've learned ch, sh, and th words with Meeble, can you work through these puzzles?

**Some consonants come in pairs that make special sounds.**

The letters **ch** do not make c and h sounds. When they are together, they sound like the ch in **chair**.

The letters **th** do not make t and h sounds. When they are together, they sound like the th in **three**.

The letters **sh** do not make s and h sounds. When they are together, they sound like the sh in **sheep**.

The letters **wh** do not make w and h sounds. When they are together, they sound like the wh in **wheel**.

# Point to the letters that spell the word.

| sh | a | n |
|----|---|---|
| wh | e | ll |

| th | u | le |
|----|---|----|
| wh | a | d |

| b | i | th |
|---|---|----|
| f | a | sh |

| r | a | sh |
|---|---|-----|
| d | i | ch |

| th | e | nk |
|----|---|----|
| sh | i | d |

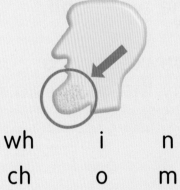

| wh | i | n |
|----|---|---|
| ch | o | m |

| sh | a | te |
|----|---|----|
| wh | i | pe |

| b | i | sh |
|---|---|----|
| w | a | th |

# Vowel Pairs

**Sometimes vowels come in pairs.**
The first one says its name and the second one listens. You say the name of the first vowel, but not the second vowel.

Look at the word **seal**.

The first vowel is an **e**.
So you say the **e** and do not say the **a**.

Look at the word **nail**.

The first vowel is an **a**.
So you say the **a** and do not say the **i**.

Look at the word **boat**.

The first vowel is an **o**.
So you say the **o** and do not say the **a**.

For each word, point to the sound that you say.

rain

jail

leaf

sea

road

goat

# Rhymes

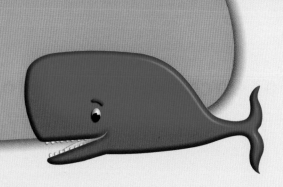

**Words that rhyme have the same ending sound.**

**Box** and **fox** rhyme. They both end in the –ox sound.

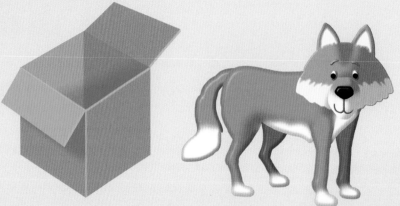

Words do not need to have the same spelling to rhyme.

**Peel** and **seal** rhyme. They are not spelled with the same ending letters, but they both end with the same –eel sound when you say them.

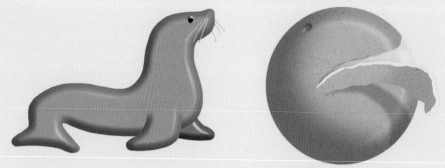

**Point to the words in
each row that rhyme.**

1. you       of       to

2. chase       cake       case

3. green       bean       bed

4. sock       block       ox

chair

5. bit       fly       tie

6. can       cap       fan

7. pair       hare       fear

8. fan       pane       rain

pair

# Color Words

**Every color has a name. Which colors are in a rainbow?**

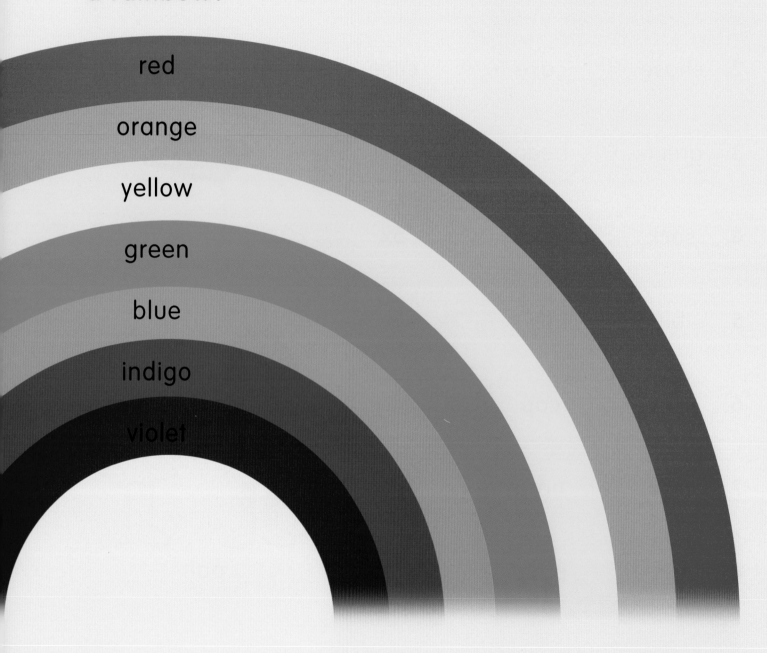

red

orange

yellow

green

blue

indigo

violet

**Word bank**

| indigo | blue | orange |
| white | green | red |
| black | yellow | brown |

If you are unsure, counting the spaces below might give you a clue!

___ ___ ___ ___ ___

___ ___ ___ ___          ___ ___ ___ ___ ___ ___

___ ___ ___ ___ ___          ___ ___ ___ ___ ___ ___

___ ___ ___ ___ ___ ___ ___ ___          ___ ___ ___ ___ ___ ___

___ ___ ___ ___ ___ ___ ___

___ ___ ___ ___ ___ ___ ___ ___

# Calendar Words

**Many words help you to tell the time.
These words are used on a calendar.**

The names of the days of the week are...

| | |
|---|---|
| Monday | Saturday |
| Tuesday | Sunday |
| Wednesday | |
| Thursday | |
| Friday | |

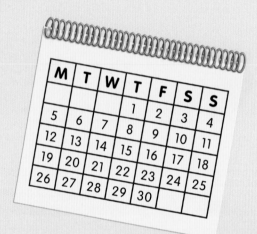

The names of the months of the year are...

| | |
|---|---|
| January | July |
| February | August |
| March | September |
| April | October |
| May | November |
| June | December |

Other words, such as yesterday, today, tomorrow, day, month and year can also help you to talk about time.

The words below are all jumbled up! Point to the days of the week, and then the months of the year, in the correct order.

Today is Monday

WEDNESDAY          SATURDAY

          MONDAY          THURSDAY

FRIDAY          SUNDAY          TUESDAY


MARCH          JUNE          SEPTEMBER          JULY

     AUGUST          DECEMBER          APRIL

          FEBRUARY          MAY          OCTOBER

NOVEMBER                    JANUARY

# Number Words

**Numbers can be written with digits.**

# 1, 2, 3, 4, 5, 6, 7, 8, 9, 10

Numbers can also be written as words.

**one, two, three, four, five, six, seven, eight, nine, ten**

**Count the number of pictures shown. Point to the correct digit and word number above.**

If you are unsure, counting the spaces below might give you a clue!

☐ _ _ _ egg

☐ _ _ _ chicks

☐ _ _ _ _ _ _ cows

☐ _ _ _ _ bales

☐ _ _ _ _ horses

☐ _ _ _ _ pigs

☐ _ _ _ _ _ _ corn ears

☐ _ _ _ _ _ cherries

☐ _ _ _ _ _ cows

☐ _ _ _ _ cats

# Here and There

Some words help tell you where you are.

**on      up      here      there      under**

Look at the picture. Point to the correct words above to finish the sentences opposite.

**If you are unsure, counting the spaces below might give you a clue!**

Where is Kitty?

She's __ __ the tree.

Where is Joe?

He's __ __ __ __ __ the seat.

Where is Clare?

She's __ __ the slide.

Has Lisa found Kitty?

Yes, __ __ __ __ she is!

Where is the school?

It's __ __ __ __ __ .

Other Titles in this Series Include:

## Fun with Words
Find out about all the different ways you can write and have some fun with words!

## Fun with Math
Discover exciting activities, with the help of some colorful characters,
and have some fun with math!

## Fun with Drawing and Painting
Find out about all the different ways you can
draw and paint and have some fun with art!

## Fun with Prints and Special Effects
Find out how to make the most of your prints and have some fun with art!